Master Hand Metal Engraving

How To Get Started

Content

Introduction

I've always been drawn to engraved metal accessories and jewelry because of the monograms, sentiments, and design elements I mentioned above. Engraving is such an elegant way to personalize jewelry. It allows us to share a message, date, or monogram worthy of being worn or displayed forever, or to add one-of-a-kind design details to metal surfaces. If you agree and are ready to learn something new this year, join me in mastering hand engraving!

I have a very dear, talented friend who is a third-generation jeweller. My heart was bursting when his mother told me a charming story about him engraving a silver platter in his grandfather's shop AT THE AGE OF 5. Years later, when he showed me his grandfather's hand-engraving tools, my eyes welled up with tears. They had a magical quality about them that can only come with age and the labor of love.

I loved knowing that he and his grandfather used those tools for hundreds of hours. Imagine all the anniversary gifts, wedding bands, watches, and other **jewellery** that was personalized using those tools. The romantic in me loves to think about how many special sentiments, notable dates, monograms, and other one-of-a-kind designs those tools created.

Chapter 1: Introduction to hand engraving

The History of Hand Engraving

Hand engraving, is the age old art form, of carving out designs and images onto a variety of mediums. Throughout human history, some form of hand engraving can be found, at times even in perfect condition, despite hundreds of years of elemental exposure. From cave walls to glass, stone to wood, and every known metal touched, this craft remains timeless.

In colonial America, hand engraving was revived by master engraver, Paul Revere. A famous silversmith, he and others of his time engraved beautiful silver and pewter pieces to display the owner's wealth. The engravings included family crests, coats of arms, monogrammed silverware, teapots and other household items.

Metal Hand Engraving is not only beautiful and worth preserving, but can also act as a personal history record, in the form of high art. A name engraved on a watch, passed down from generation to generation. Recognition of a new life, added to the recorded family tree. Or a secret, carved within the gold rings of two lovers. Hand engraving is an everlasting mark on history.

With such a rich history and a unique specialist skill, you may wonder why there aren't more Engravers. Firstly it takes 3-5 years of training to become a hand engraver, secondly the introduction of laser and machine engraving has increased its usage in commercial engraving, reducing the availability of hand engraving training. Hand engraving remains a specialist art form, traditionally reserved for luxury brands but we believe in making the fine jewellery making industry more accessible, which is why we offer technical training and equip the next generation of craftsmen and women with traditional skills.

What is jewellery engraving?

The term engraving can be defined in one of two ways:

An engraving is a picture or design that has been cut into a surface.

An engraving is a picture that has been printed from a plate on which designs have been cut.

The history of engraving can be traced as far back as Roman times, and is a technique which requires a great deal of skill and patience. Traditionally, engraving was used to create images on metal plates or wooden blocks which were then used for printing. However, it is also a form of decoration for metal objects and jewellery which can be used to provide texture, imagery and most commonly lettering to pieces which would otherwise be plain.

What is hand engraving?

Hand engraving is carried out using shaped steel cutters with a sharpened edge which are mounted into a wooden handle. The cutters themselves are supplied in extra-long lengths, so that they can be cut down to suit the person using them. The 'tang' (pointed handle end) is not as hard as the jewellery engraving tool itself, and is intended to be snapped off to create the ideal length. This rough end should be ground down and inserted into a wooden handle ready for use during hand engraving.

Square-Shaped Hand Engraving Tool

Square Graver

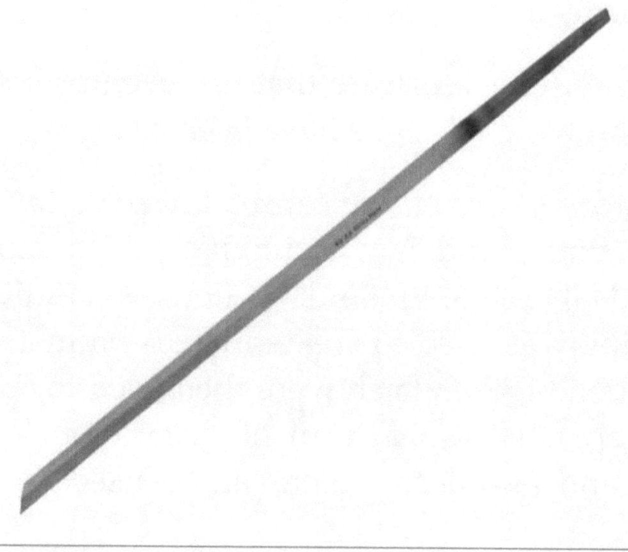

Chapter 2: How to engrave at home using hand engraving tools

Jewellery engraving designs can be drawn directly onto metal or transferred using a variety of methods. As you start to trace your first line, your hand engraving tool should be pushed down and forward with even pressure. The process is repeated until the required depth of each cut is reached.

Your hand engraving tools should be held at an angle which is neither too deep nor too shallow, but, only experience and practice will help you when learning how to engrave metal by hand. You'll find that there is a variety of tools available for jewellery engraving. For beginners, it's best to use more basic jewellery tools for example, a v-shaped graver or knife graver.

Different types of hand engraving tools

Here's some of the steel hand engraving tools you can use:

Scraper – used to scrape away the metal surface to clean it.

Spit stick – used to cut fluid lines.

Scorper – used to cut and carve larger areas of metal away. Available in a range of different profiles: flat, round edge, oval, onglette, etc. each producing a shaped cut.

Graver – used to cut lines that swell or shrink in metal depending on the angle used. Used in stone setting and jewellery engraving and available in a range of differently shaped profiles: knife, chisel, square, diamond, flat edge, round edge, oval etc.

How the Engraving Tool Works

Engraving tools are miniature chisels made of hardened steel. In proper engraving a sharpened tool is set against the metal at a specific angle and pressure applied both downward and forward. The tool buries itself into the sheet, forms a chip, and pushes that curl of metal ahead of it as it cuts.

The angle of attack is important to achieve a controlled and uniform cut. If the angle is too steep the tool digs itself into the sheet making it impossible to push it forward. The effort to overpower a buried tool can result in a loss of control and a broken tip. If the angle is too shallow the point never gains purchase on the sheet. There is no chip formed and no cut made. Because the tip of the tool is not caught by the metal, the tool easily slips, creating a nasty scratch.

The proper angle will depend on the shape of the graver, the quality of the desired line and the metal being cut. Understanding and responding to these factors requires a sensitive touch and considerable experience.

Engraving Tool Shapes

Engraving tools, called gravers, are precise instruments. They must be made from top quality steel, shaped and sharpened to specific angles, and fitted into handles that provide comfort and control. Commercially available gravers are made from a highly refined fine grained tool steel. A high speed steel is to be recommended for working harder materials and to have the greatest possible durability; there are even engraving tools with carbide cutting tips.

Gravers are usually sold with preshaped tips, but these angles will need to be reworked before the tool is used. Gravers can be purchased from jewelry supply companies in the shapes shown in figure

10.21.

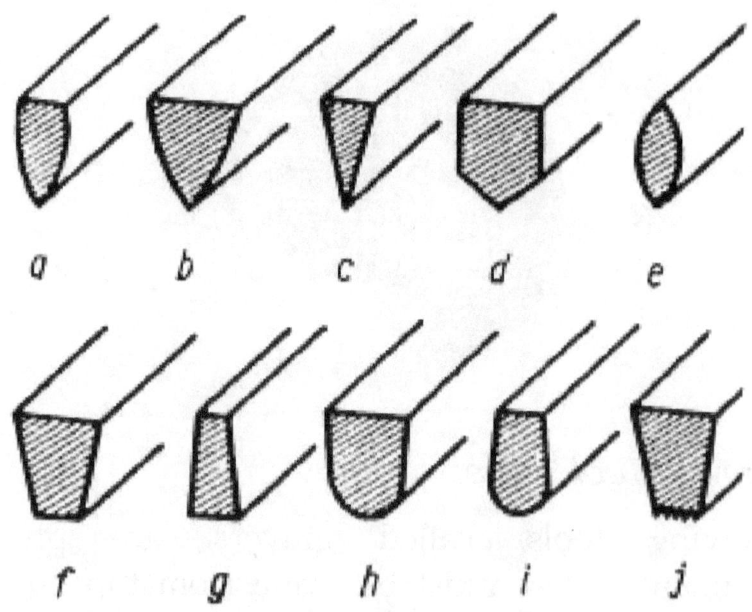

Gravers forms.

a) small pointed (onglette) graver.

b) wider pointed graver

c) knife graver

d) facet graver

e) ovel graver

f) flat gracer with wide rib

g) flat graver with small rib

h) rounded grave

i) rounded graver with small rib

j) line graver

Onglette

This popular shape is shown in two sizes in 10.21a and 10.21b. The sides curve slightly outward from a top edge that is flat and can range from one to four millimeters wide. This tool offers great versatility, cutting a thin line with a light stroke and widening as it is rolled on its side or pressed more deeply into the sheet. It is preferred for cutting letters because of the ease with which it cuts a line of increasing width.

Knife Graver

Illustrated at 10.21c, this graver is a slim, straight-walled version of the onglette. It is difficult to control on curves and rarely used by itself, but it cuts deep hair-thin lines. It is often used to add delicate embellishments to figures cut with other tools.

Beveled Graver

This is the stout sibling of the wide onglette, figure 10.21d, used to make bold cuts in tough metal. The side surfaces

form an angle of 100¡, with the upper sides being parallel. The width of the back can be between 1.5-3 mm.

Oval Graver

This tool, shown at 10.21e can be considered a slim version of the onglette, but in this case the pointed oval is not truncated with a flat spine along the top. In practice this shape offers a blank that is ground as needed to create a tool to shave metal from within tight enclosures. This is the tool, for instance, that is used to carve a seat for a stone inside a bezel wall.

Flat Graver

This tool has a flat base, or ÒbellyÓ that can be used to carve away unwanted metal, as for instance when removing excess solder. The cross section can be trapezoidal (figure 10.21f and g) or a rectangle (not shown). This is also the tool used to make decorative wiggle cuts. It is the practical workhorse of the graver family, being used less for ornamentation than shaving, scraping, and cutting textures. Flat gravers are available in widths from 0.2 mm to 5 mm.

Round Graver

This name is deceiving because the tool itself, pictured in two sizes at 10.21h and 10.21j, is not round. Nevertheless, the groove it cuts is a round-bottomed trench and it is from this the name is derived. As shown, the side walls can be either parallel or sloped. This tool is among the easiest to control and is therefore useful for all kinds of decorative work.

Florentine Finish Graver

This tool looks at first glance like a flat graver, but closer examination will reveal delicate lines cut lengthwise into the belly. These cut fine parallel lines into the surface, an effect that is used to ornament an otherwise plain surface while simultaneously protecting it from wear and fingerprints.

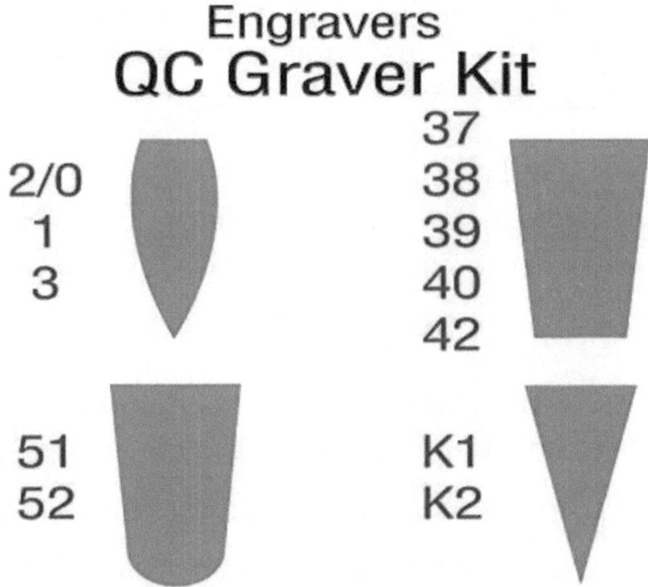

Chapter 3: What is the difference between hand engraving and machine engraving?

Hand engraving can be done with either hand tools or a rotary tool to create unique designs of various depths. Machine engraving uses a laser to burn designs into a surface, and while the results are clean and precise, the cuts are often quite shallow.

Those new to the hobby have several options as far as engraving methods are concerned, and choosing the right one can be admittedly confusing.

Let's look carefully at what hand engraving entails and the machine engraving options available today so you can decide which method is right for you.

Hand Engraving Methods

There's nothing quite like the satisfaction of creating something with your own two hands.

Engraving items by hand ensures truly unique results and is arguably the best approach for adding a personal touch to items made from a variety of materials.

I go into more detail about what items can be engraved here, but for now, know that it is possible to engrave wood, glass, plastic, leather, metal, pottery, and even stone with simple hand-engraving techniques.

Hand engraving allows artists to creatively express themselves while enjoying the pleasure that comes from working with their hands.

Traditionally, hand engraving was performed using only non-electric hand tools, such as gravers, chisels, and gouges, depending on the material being engraved.

Surface material is methodically removed, bit by bit, until the chosen design is complete.

The invention of the first rotary tool in 1935, aptly named the Multi-tool and later the Moto-tool, revolutionized the world of hand engraving.

This simple, compact rotary tool can be used to sand, polish, cut, grind, drill, saw, and yes, even engrave.

With this handy, multipurpose tool, engravers can now enjoy the best of both worlds – working with their hands and benefiting from labor-saving devices that produce accurate results.

Of course, some crafters prefer to stick with the old-school hand tools.

Others find that employing the use of a simple, handheld machine provides more accurate results in less time while still qualifying as hand engraving, and thus, is the superior method.

You, however, will have to decide for yourself.

Using Only Hand Tools

There are plenty of people who choose to forego all forms of modern technology when it comes to engraving.

Wood, metal, plastic, leather, and stone can all be engraved with a few simple hand tools, a steady hand, and plenty of patience.

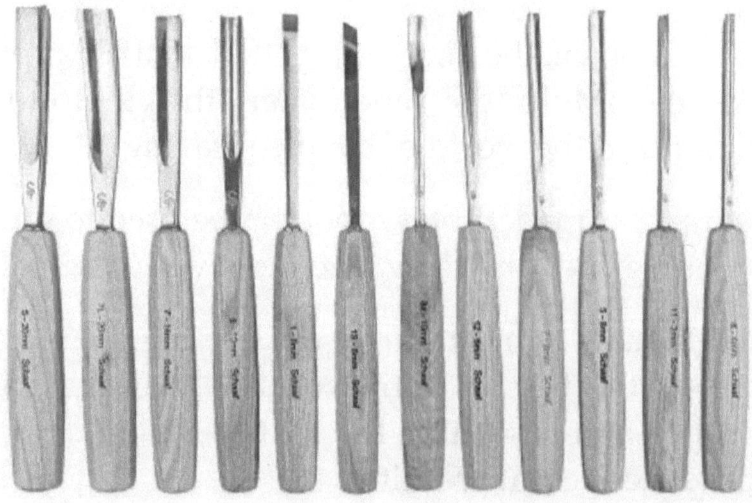

While a quality set of chisels and gouges, like my favorite Schaaf wood carving set, is really all that is needed for carving wood, for harder materials, like metal, you'll need to use gravers, also called burins, in a variety of sizes.

Advantages:

Quiet work environment without any noisy machinery.

Each engraving will be unique.

Less dust and small, potentially harmful particles are produced.

Can be done on heat-sensitive materials, like plastic.

Tools last a long time if cared for well.

Deep engravings are possible.

Disadvantages:

This method will take the longest time.

Large projects can be tedious and hard on your hands.

Mistakes can be easily made.

Rough cuts may be visible (slight imperfections are common).

Requires skill and can take years to truly master.

Edges may be rough and require smoothing.

Tools must be sharpened routinely.

Using a Rotary Tool

A rotary tool is by far the most common way home crafters engrave items. Depending on your skill level, designs can be completed in mere minutes, and, as when using hand tools, many materials, such as wood, plastic, leather, and stone can be engraved.

However, because of the gentle rotary action as opposed to the forceful chiseling of hand tools, even more delicate materials like glass and pottery can be engraved with a rotary tool.

As long as you have the correct burrs for the job at hand, either tungsten carbide or diamond tip depending on the material's hardness, an ordinary rotary tool, such as this one by Wen (I use my mine all the time for household jobs) will be all that you need.

However, there are also rotary tools made specifically for engraving. Most of these models are made with comfort in mind and come with everything you need to get started.

Some, like the Original Easy Etcher, look much like a pen but are powerful enough to engrave even hard materials, like metal.

Other models are a bit larger but can perform all of the same functions of regular rotary tool.

Personally, I think I would go with the Uolor Engraving Kit, just because it comes with so many accessories and bits/burrs, but the Utool Engraver is another excellent option, complete with everything you need

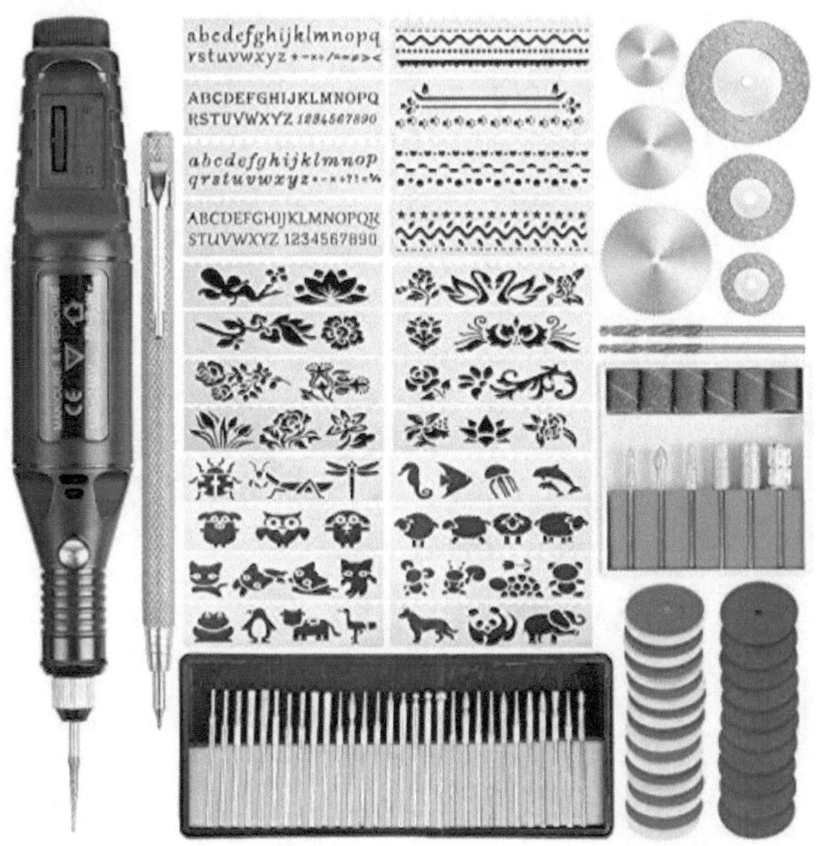

Advantages:

Engraves a wide variety of materials.

Can be used on more delicate materials, such as glass and pottery.

Interchangeable bits allow for different effects and cutting possibilities.

Most have several speed/depth settings.

Comfortable to hold and easy to use (similar to writing by hand).

With practice, precise results are possible.

Disadvantages:

Some models are rather noisy.

Produces saw dust (if used on wood) and other particles – a mask should be worn during use.

Mastering control will take practice.

Machine Engraving

Over the past few decades, the popularity of laser machines has skyrocketed.

Several men, including Bill Lawson and Tom Zarden, are credited with advancing laser technology to make it suitable for engraving work.

Today, laser engraved items are commonplace, and the array of images and artwork that can be reproduced onto nearly any surface is nothing short of astounding.

How Do Laser Engraving Machines Work?

Laser engraving machines utilize massive levels of focused energy to remove surface layers from various materials by literally vaporizing the particles.

In most cases, designs are sent to the machine from a computer, though smaller machines only call for an app installed on your phone.

The laser machine "reads" the design, and the laser burns away layers to replicate the design exactly.

Large laser engraving machines can cost a small fortune, but a hobbyist engraver wouldn't have much use for equipment of that size anyway.

Smaller, portable desktop versions are a much better option for those wishing to occasionally engrave relatively soft materials, such as plastic, wood, paper, and leather.

For those who have never experimented with a laser machine before, I have two recommendations.

Both are easy to use, yield great results, and are small enough that they won't dominate the room. Just be mindful of their limitations, as they are not large, industrial machines.

The Twotrees DIY Engraver Kit sits on a sturdy,

horizontal frame and is capable of both engraving and cutting.

Designs as large as 30 by 40 centimeters in size can be easily and quickly engraved on wood, leather, plastic, paper, and bamboo.

The Laserpecker Desktop Engraver is controlled by a phone app and is easily positioned on any flat surface, or you can utilize the included tripod for more angles when engraving hard-to-position items.

Like the Twotrees Engraver, this model works best on fairly soft materials.

Advantages:

High level of accuracy.

Most machines will only engrave flat surfaces.

Smooth edges and crisp, clean engravings.

Very fast.

Uniform result for mass production.

Disadvantages:

Lacks individuality.

Grooves are typically quite shallow.

Small models cannot be used on metal, stone, glass, and other hard materials.

Depending on the material, fumes may be dangerous.

Due to the lack of depth, engravings may not last as long as with other methods.

Chapter 4: Preparation of the Engraving Tool

It is customary that graver blanks are furnished in a length sufficient to accommodate the largest hand. This means that the rest of us must start by shortening them. Grasp the tool vertically in a vise with the unwanted portion of the tang projecting up. Strike a vigorous blow with a steel hammer sideways against the tang and it will snap off cleanly. To prevent the tip from shooting across the room, catch the broken off part in a towel or rag held against the vise.

Reshape the tang by grinding, either with a bench grinder, sanding machine, or appropriate wheels on a flexible shaft machine. The graver is secured by friction into a handle in the same manner as a file; secure it into a vise and tap the handle into place with a mallet. As the tool becomes shorter through numerous sharpenings, a long handle is replaced by a shorter one. Though the grip might feel a little awkward at first, it will become more comfortable with experience. If your hand muscles get cramped during engraving the tool is too short and should be replaced.

Proper shaping and sharpening of gravers is as important as it is difficult to describe on the printed page. The following description should be supplemented with practice and experimentation.

Refer to figure 10.22, an onglette graver, for the following instructions. In general these same steps will be used for other shapes, though the angles of each tool differ slightly.

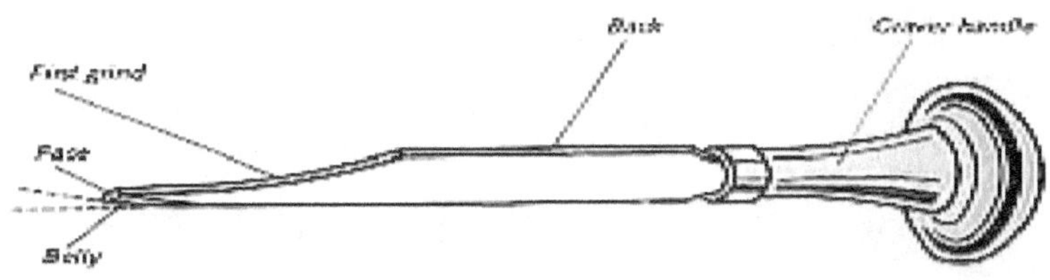

Gravers are sold in their hardened state and any grinding should be done in such a way that this temper is preserved. Touch the tool lightly to the grinding wheel, dipping it frequently into water throughout the process to prevent it from overheating. If the steel starts to show color the temper has been compromised.

The first step is to narrow the area adjacent to the tip for 1-2 centimeters (1/2 – 3/4 inch). This will allow better viewing of the working tip of the tool and facilitate sharpening since there is less metal to be removed. Use a stone to cut away at least half of the top section at the tip, creating a gentle arc as shown. This edge should be made smooth because your fingers will be resting on it while cutting. Do not go too far back because this will weaken the tool.

The belly or underside of the graver is ground so it

shows two symmetrical facets. If the tool was turned over, these might be said to resemble the roof of a house. The angle between these two facets will be between 30 and 60° depending upon the hardness of the material to be cut. A narrow tip cuts a finer line but is more fragile.

The face of the tool is then ground to a slope, typically around 45°, again depending on the material being cut; the finer the slope, the more delicate the tool. It might help to visualize a pencil point. If it is made very long and pointy it makes a fine line but often breaks in use.

Both belly and face surfaces should be perfectly flat like the facets on a gem. This will insure that the angles where the faces meet are straight and crisp, which in turn is what makes the tool sharp. Grinding is usually done on an oilstone, working in a circular stroke, first on a coarse stone and then on a finer one. When the surfaces are correct – check with magnification – shift to a polishing stone like Arkansas or a fine abrasive paper. Follow this with a few strokes on a hard leather with a polishing powder to create a mirror bright finish.

Test the sharpening by sliding the tip of the graver along your thumb nail. A properly sharpened tool will stick immediately while an improperly shaped tool will slide off. There is no point in going to the metal until the tool passes this test. Cutting with a dull graver is tedious, uncontrolled and almost certain to ruin the work.

Uolor 108 Pcs Engraving Tool Kit

Multi-Functional Electric Corded Micro Engraver Etching Pen DIY Rotary Tool for Jewelry Glass Wood Metal Ceramic Plastic with Scriber, 82 Accessories and 24 Stencils

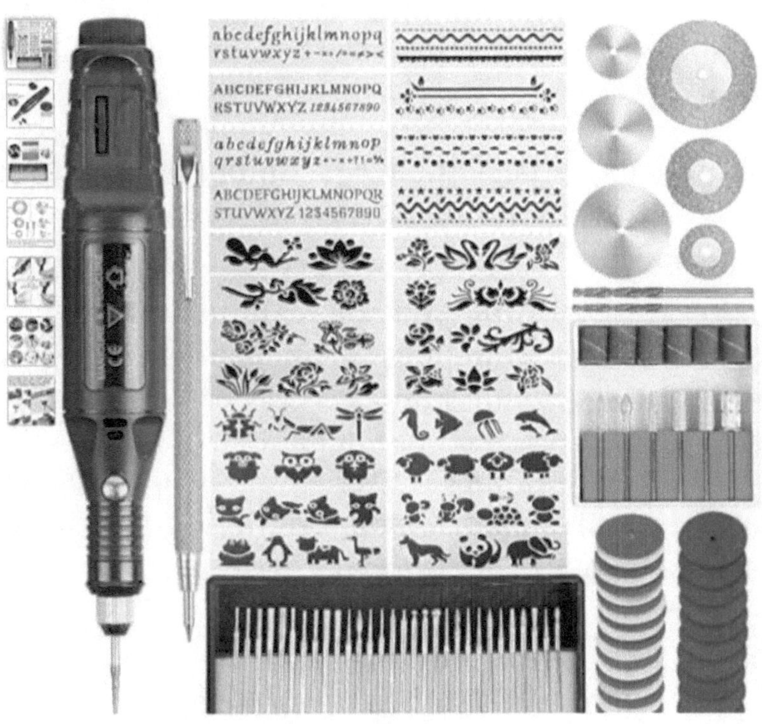

▲Get an engraving kit that does it all. This unique kit lets you engrave personalize or decorate almost any surface in seconds - metal, plastic, glass, ceramic, wood, leather, diamond, stone and more. It's perfect for small light job like DIY Creation, Crafting, Lightweight Projects.

▲2 in 1 rotary button controls ON/OFF and stepless speed from 3,000 to 20,000 RPM (Revolutions per Minute) for different materials

▲82 Accessories and Scriber Included - The rotary DIY tool kit includes all kinds of accessories can widely be used in Engraving, Carving, Sanding, Polishing, Etching, Routing, Grinding, Drilling, Cutting etc.

▲24 Stencils - 4 basic Letter/Number templates help etch words and numbers. Write personal messages on jewelry or stone, or use it for engraving personalized arts and crafts. 4 Graphic, 8 Flower and 8 Lovely Animal stencils give you more ways to personalize your valuables

▲Light and compact pen-like design provides comfortable use for precision engraving performance from fine lines to deep grooves. Ergonomic grip adds extra comfort and steady control

Chapter 5: The art of Hand Engraving Jewellery

Hand engraving of jewelry is a very skilled technique used to carve precious metal, creating lettering or intricate designs of decorative jewelry art. These techniques have existed since the times of ancient Egypt, and were refined in the 15th century by German goldsmiths.

A hand engraver is a highly skilled artisan who uses a small wooden-handled steel tool (known as a burin or graver) to carve or "cut" into the surface of the metal, cutting to various depths to achieve the desired design. This hand-carved quality catches the light in a unique manner. The fine lines or cuts are used like a graphic artist might use pen and ink to make fine lines or calligraphy on paper. A skilled hand engraver can do a variety of patterns and images on any surface of a piece of precious metal.

Tools and Techniques of a skilled hand engraver

Hand engraving happens in a studio environment., similar to a jeweler's studio but specialized for the engraving process. On a bench top the engraver usually holds the piece to be engraved in an engraver's block, which is a heavy steel ball that has a clamp to hold the work in place. This gives the engraver a movable, but solid grip on a smaller piece and frees both hands for working.

The engraver then marks his design in pencil or ink and uses a steel tool to carve lines and shapes into the surface of the metal object he is working on.

Almost all jewelry engravers today use a power-assisted tool for their "hand" engraving. Our engraver is old-school, engraving since 1970 using similar tools to those used in the 1500s. He is one of the last practitioners of the great hand engraving tradition.

What can be hand engraved? It's not just for jewelry...

Anything metal can be engraved. Hand engravers can work on fine jewelry made in different metals as well as guns and trophies. Many famous sporting competitions have grand trophies that are hand engraved with emblems and the people's names who won the competition. The Stanley Cup and the Indy 500 Trophy are just two examples of hand-engraving. They are amazing works of craftsmanship.

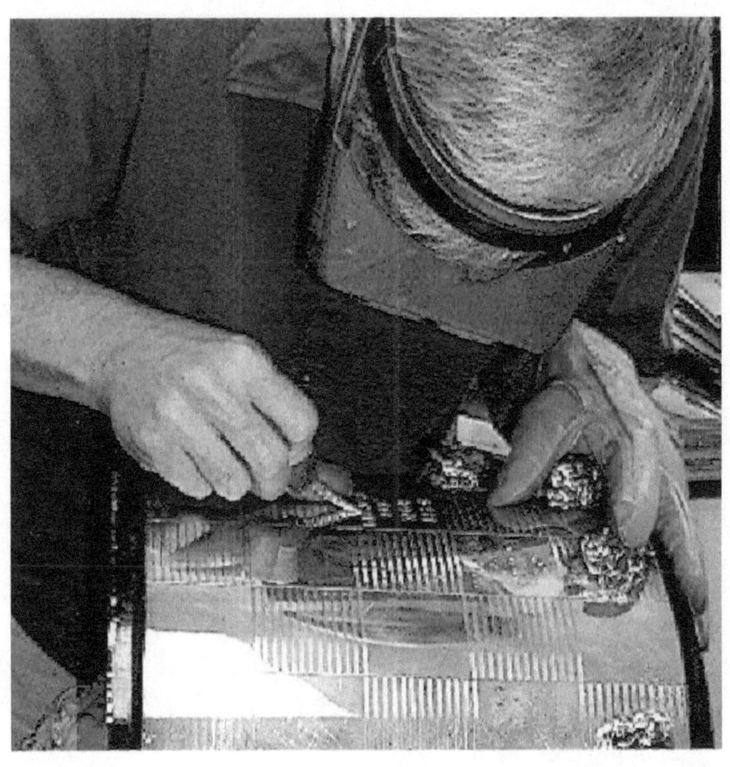

Let's take a closer look at our specialty, hand engraving for custom jewelry design!

Hand engraving on fine jewelry can be on the outside surface or in the case of a ring or bracelet on the inside surface. Inside ring inscriptions are wonderful personalizations that can date a ring to its original owner, sometimes decades earlier. It's wonderful to read an old set of initials or dates that belong to an ancestor who passed the ring on. It's a great connection and tradition.

Beautiful Textures and Patterns

There is such beauty in well-crafted hand engraving. There is no other way to achieve the same appearance in fine jewelry. Hand engraving adds texture to the metal that glistens and shimmers in the light, revealing the patterns used to create the design.

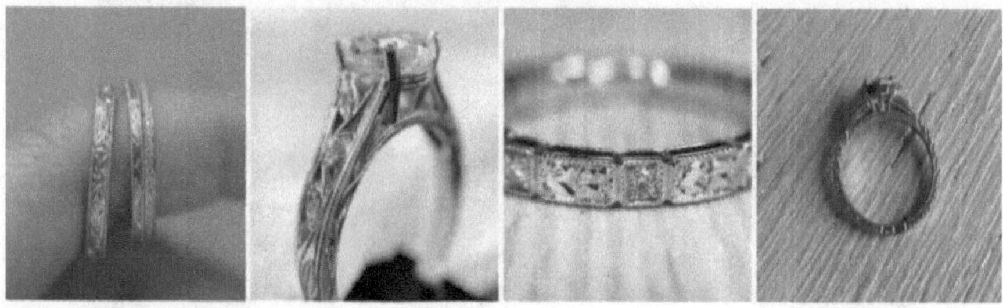

Each of the rings also has mill grained edges. Many of the vintage patterns are inspired by nature and repeated motifs.

Here is a combination of hand engraved details and milgrain for a vintage style.

This vintage style wedding ring has round brilliant diamonds set at intervals in between panels of hand engraved patterns.

This vintage style has a lovely and intricate hand carved design.

Hand engraving has a sublime quality. Each established master of hand engraving has a personality to their work. After years of practice and concentration, each engraver's work has a voice that is uniquely their own, like an artist's signature brush stroke. This uniqueness adds character to each piece produced.

With new technology and the desire to reduce expenses, by reducing skilled labor, other types of engraving have been invented. Laser engraving is sometimes used in jewelry creation, but it has none of the character of hand engraving. Simple (mechanical style) Machine engraving is also used in jewelry creation, especially for inside ring lettering engraving. It serves a purpose, but has a printed look unlike the handwritten calligraphy look of true hand engraving. Sometimes in lower-end jewelry hand engraving is simulated by making textures in models before casting them in metal, thereby saving the time to do it in actual metal. This is an inexpensive, poor imitation of true hand engraving and laks the subtle texture needed to give hand engraving it's telltale appearance.

A Time-honored Tradition

Hand engraving is both a craft and an art form. It takes many years to master, and there are very few master engravers working today. Like watchmakers or any other endangered trade, there is real danger of losing this skill to history. Hopefully, the appreciation of this art will endure and give value to craftsmen (and women) who continue this craft.

Chapter 6: Ten common mistakes made by beginners

1.) POOR FORM - If you're right-handed, the graver should be held in the right hand with the tool cutting from east to west, since the tool naturally points in that direction when held correctly. Quite often beginners will attempt to engrave from south to north. This is poor form and control is very difficult to maintain. Left handers should cut from west to east. The tool is held stationary and the vise rotates into the tool.

2.) FOOT PEDAL ERRORS - The handpiece should not be stroking until the tool is placed on the metal. Attempting to accurately place a running handpiece onto the surface of your work is an exercise in frustration. Don't press the foot pedal until the tool is in place and ready to cut.

3.) VISE ROTATION ERRORS - The vise can only be rotated as far as the left hand comfortably turn it. At this point you should stop your handpiece and reposition your left hand on the vise, then resume cutting. If the handpiece contiues to run while you reposition your hand, irregularities and flat spots on what should be smooth curves will occur. I realize that when you stop a cut in progress and then start again you run the risk of having what I call a stop-and-start spot in your line. You will overcome this with practice.

4.) LACK OF BACK-CUTTING - When a graver enters the metal it produces a tapered start before it reaches desired width. For many things such as shading, this tapering is very desirable. For many other things this tapered end makes the work look unfinished. For instance, the corners of a border should have a clean, crisp intersection. Neglecting to back-cut areas like this says you're either in a hurry to finish the job or you don't really care how it looks. It only takes a few seconds to a 1000% difference. Do it. Back-cutting should also be done on block lettering.

5.) BADLY SHAPED SCROLLS - The backbone line

of a scroll should faithfully follow the perfect spiraling proportion of the chambered nautilus shell. The number of turns of a scroll is a matter of personal preferance, but the proportion should be rigidly adhered to. The engraver

should take as much time as necessary to draw correctly proportioned backbone lines. This line is the most important line in your scrollwork, and defines the quality of the design. You can have the best tool control and do the finest shading in the world, but if the scrolls are not executed with correct proportion, the quality suffers

severely.

6.) INCORRECT MICROSCOPE SETUP - Set eyepieces to zero. Zoom scope to maximum magnification. Focus. Zoom scope to lowest magnification. Adjust eyepiece focus if needed. Not following this procedure results in an out-of-focus microscope each time it's zoomed, causing frustration and lost time.

7.) CENTERING VISE FOR MICROSCOPE USE - The area you're engraving MUST be under the microscope's objective lens. If you use the GRS Turntable base, be sure to use the centering post to place the microscope over the center of the turntable's rotation. Once centering has been established, lock the microscope into position and don't move it. Chasing the work around with the microscope is frustrating and costs you a tremendous amount of lost time. If you're using another turntable base, do whatever necessary to place the microscope directly over its center of rotation and then lock it down. This is extremely important. Don't make the mistake of not keeping your work properly centered.

8.) INCORRECT HANDPIECE TUNING - The air pressure must be adjusted correctly for optimum handpiece performance. If the air pressure is to high, the foot pedal must depressed too far before the handpiece begins tapping. This makes a hissing sound from the pedal and results in poor handpiece performance. Increasing the air pressure only makes the problem worse. Too little air pressure causes excessive handpiece vibration with little or no usable performance.

Tuning procedure: Lower the air pressure to zero. Hold the handpiece upright in your left hand while you increase the air pressure by adjusting the regulator with your right hand. You will feel the handpiece begin to flutter and then begin tapping as you increase pressure. Keep going until the tapping stops. This procedure tunes the handpiece with the foot throttle for optimum performance, so there is no foot pedal travel before the handpiece starts tapping. If you have a GraverMach, even finer tuning can be achieved with the Bias control.

9.) WORKING WITH DULL GRAVERS - If you notice a change in graver performance or behavior, chances are you need to resharpen. If you have a microscope, zoom to maximum magnification and inspect the point of the tool. If the point is broken or appears dull, resharpen the face and heel. Continuing to engrave with a dull tool only frustrates the engraver and the quality of the work suffers. If you're unsure if the tool is dull, then resharpen. Sometimes a dull or broken graver can be difficult for an inexperienced engraver to detect.

10.) DEBURRING WORK - The inexperienced engraver will quite often produce engraving that feels rough to the touch, as they haven't developed the graver control and finesse of more experienced engravers (don't worry, it'll come). If you pass your finger across your finished work and feel sharp burs, then the work must be lightly sanded by 2000 grit (or finer) abrasive paper. I caution you about sanding your engraving because it's very easy to spoil good work. It should be kept to an absolute minimum, and done BEFORE the final shading lines are cut. If you sand shaded work, you will certainly wreck many hours of labor with a few passes of sandpaper. Debur your work once it's outlined and/or the background has been removed, and bring to a final finish and stop. After the shading is done, no further sanding should be done. I should note that there's nothing wrong with feeling sharp, crisp engraving, but a rough surface with burs definitely needs attenti on. Quite often individual burs can be carefully trimmed off with a graver under high power magnification. If you've blackened your finished engraving, burs and rough edges can hold paint, and this can make the finished work look quite bad.

Though the decision is yours, most people opt for hand engraving with a rotary tool because it can be used on so many materials, is easy to learn and use, and is capable of producing engravings of various depths.